Small Business Failures

Solopreneurs and Self-Employed
Consultants Need to Avoid!

Heidi Thorne

Copyright 2016 Heidi Thorne
All rights reserved.
ISBN: 1537373269
ISBN-13: 978-1537373263

All rights reserved. No part of this publication may be reproduced, stored in a retrieval system, or transmitted in any form or by any means, electronic, mechanical, recording or otherwise, without the prior written permission of the author and publisher.

Disclaimer: Heidi Thorne, Thorne Communications LLC, any of its affiliates, and any of its or its affiliate's respective shareholders, directors, officers, employees, agents, representatives, successors or assigns (collectively, "Thorne") does not make any guarantee or other promises as to any results that may be achieved or obtained through your use of the product you've purchased (the "Product") or any information or materials presented therewith, provided in connection therewith or included therein. The information provided in the Product and any accompanying material is for informational purposes only, and should not be used as a substitute for your own research and due diligence. Your use of the Product is at your own risk. You are responsible for checking with appropriate authorities to ensure compliance with all applicable laws and regulations.

Without limiting the foregoing, Thorne hereby disclaims any and all representations and warranties with respect to the Product, including, without limitation, any representation and warranty with respect to the achievement of any results, the correctness or completeness of any information or materials presented with the Product, provided in connection with the Product or included in the Product or the advisability of any act or failure to act. You acknowledge and agree that Thorne shall have no liability or obligation to you or any of your affiliates or any of your or your affiliate's respective shareholders, directors, officers, employees, agents, representatives, successors or assigns for any claims, damages, expenses or other losses arising out of, in connection with, resulting from or otherwise relating to the Product, including, without limitation, any errors or omissions therein.

First Edition, August 2016

Thorne Communications LLC, USA
www.ThorneCommunications.com

Small Business Failures

Solopreneurs and Self-Employed Consultants Need to Avoid!

Heidi Thorne

Table of Contents

Been There, Done That ix

IDENTITY CRISIS 1

    Chapter 1: The "Lemonade Stand"........................3

    Chapter 2: Unicorns...8

    Chapter 3: One-Trick Pony...................................12

    Chapter 4: Superhero..15

    Chapter 5: The Accidental Charity 21

BOUNDARY BLUNDERS 27

    Chapter 6: Bandwidth Bandits...........................29

    Chapter 7: Time Thieves 34

    Chapter 8: Cold Pizza 38

    Chapter 9: *"I Can Also Do That"* 43

    Chapter 10: Too Many Choices..........................47

    Chapter 11: Muddled Streams of Income 52

    Chapter 12: When Clients are Friends.............57

    Chapter 13: The Price is Wrong 62

GOING FORWARD 67

    Chapter 14: Knowing When to Call in Help 69

    Add Heidi to Your Network!................................74

Been There, Done That

I wish I was writing this from the perspective of not having experienced small business failure. Sadly, that's not the case.

While much of what contributes to any small business' success or failure can be beyond our control, I've found that there are key attitudes and behaviors—particularly as they relate to how we view ourselves and how we set boundaries and expectations—that can directly and dramatically impact our finances and future as solopreneurs and consultants.

In this book, I've collected some of the blunders I've either experienced myself or observed in my network over the years. You may even see some of your own issues mirrored in the pages that follow.

What I hope you'll gain from this book is a new perspective on how you are building and managing your one-person empire.

Wishing you the best of success,
Heidi Thorne

IDENTITY CRISIS

Chapter 1:
The "Lemonade Stand"

In addition to the return of robins and green grass, the dawn of spring brings another stream of new small businesses. What businesses are those? Kids' lemonade stands.

Whenever I run across these pint-sized "kidpreneurs," it makes me smile. I always wonder if they'll actually learn anything from their experience about opening and owning a business. Sadly, though, many of them that get bitten by the entrepreneurial bug as adults may treat their real small businesses like their little lemonade empires.

Here's what happens when small business ideas take on lemonade stand business strategies...

Selling to Anyone and No One

"Wanna buy some lemonade?" a little lemonade CEO yells from across the street. Of course, I'm not interested. One, I'm usually walking my large active dogs which makes it a trick to purchase and drink it. Next, lemonade often sets my teeth on edge.

You have to cut the little Lemonade Barons and Baronesses some slack for trying. But when they grow up and open a real business, we might find them doing the same thing, screaming their marketing messages and offers to anyone with a pulse within earshot, and then wonder why their business is failing.

Proximity does not equal possibility when it comes to prospects. You need to set up your stand where thirsty people hang out which, these days, could be offline or online. And those can't be just any people. They need to be people for whom your "lemonade" would be a thirst quenching choice.

Where a business is located can make or break it. Yet many small businesses position themselves where it's convenient or cheap, but where getting traffic (the foot or Internet kind) is either impossible or expensive. For the kids, that might be mom and dad's house. Okay, we understand that's their only choice. But I once went to a cocktail party at a micro winery that was in the middle of a seedy industrial area. News flash: The wine tasting crowd ain't hanging out there.

Moving Beyond the Lemonade Stand: When opening a business offline or online, find out who wants your "lemonade" and locate where they hang out.

Sell or Swim?

Ever notice that kids' neighborhood lemonade stands are usually only in business for a couple of days before they close up shop? They don't do business in the rain, when a cool wind comes through or when the community swimming pool is calling their names. What if I really was looking for a sip of lemonade while I walked down their block?

The kids are in business as long as it's fun, makes some coin and they don't have anything better to do. Ever see some small business owners act the same way? I have. When owning and running a business gets too difficult, they get out. Though many "funpreneurs" would really be better off going out of business, many real life adult business owners give up just before their businesses turn the profit corner.

Granted, there are times when it is necessary to close a business, or a portion of it, that is not bringing in revenue and profits or just costs too much to operate. That's where sales forecasting and monitoring are so crucial. Armed with this data, an owner can make a more informed decision about the future of the business... other than basing it on that it is no longer fun.

Moving Beyond the Lemonade Stand: Know why you're in business and make a commitment to see it through the inevitable ups and downs until it reaches the end of its life cycle, becomes too unprofitable or there are other serious issues making it unwise to continue.

Cash Flow and Go

"Mom, can I make some lemonade to sell?"

"Sure, Honey. Everything's in the kitchen. Do you need some help?"

Wow, I bet many business owners would love to be able to ask "mom" for all the bits, pieces and labor that go into setting up and running a business. Most of us know that "mom" isn't there for us. But there are small business owners and entrepreneurs who rush headlong into going into business for themselves without ever researching or understanding all the costs of being in business. Materials, labor, insurance, accounting... the list is endless.

Why would they do this? Often these folks are employment "refugees" who desperately want to be in business on their own, so much so that they will ignore many of these factors. Before long, they realize the gravity of their situation and fret about the cash flow becoming cash "go."

Moving Beyond the Lemonade Stand: Understand your business costs BEFORE going into business.

Mixing Friendship and Finances

"Hey, Mister, how about buying some lemonade?"

"Aw, you're so cute. Why not?"

One of the advantages lemonade kidpreneurs have is that they can sell on being adorable. Their unique sales proposition is that they are cute and their customers usually are friends, relatives and neighbors who know, like and trust them. Sort of sounds like social media, eh?

But what happens when the kids grow up, get acne and friends and neighbors get tired of buying the same darn lemonade year after year? You guessed it. The business fails.

Yet haven't we all encountered small business folks who sell based solely on friendship? Haven't you purchased products or services based simply on the friendship factor? We all have at some point. Gets pretty uncomfortable for sellers when friends quit buying and quit connecting because they don't want to get roped into buying something else they don't really want or need.

Those friends are afraid that every call is actually a disguised sales pitch. Ugh!

While friendship can help facilitate many a sale, having limited offerings and going to the friendship well for prospects too often will torpedo any business.

Moving Beyond the Lemonade Stand: Understand the target market and its demographics to avoid uncomfortably mixing friendship and finances.

The Bottom Line

Time to grow up and grow your business!

Chapter 2:
Unicorns

I'm a big fan of the *History Channel* shows, *American Pickers* and *Pawn Stars*. One of the most interesting and entertaining aspects of the shows for me is watching how sellers value the unique (or not so unique) items they're offering for sale to the shows' stars.

Usually, a deal doesn't get done because:

• Seller is emotionally attached to the item and is setting the price based on the unique emotional value it has for them.

• Sellers have seen something "for sale on the Internet" and believe that someone else's asking price is the price they will get.

• Sellers don't realize they are selling for resale. Except in rare instances, the shows' stars are only purchasing items to sell again to others and they must make a profit.

• Sellers have an extremely rare item and equate rarity with value and price.

So what does this have to do with sales for small businesses? Most of these deal breakers mirror challenges with managing a business' uniqueness and competitive advantage. Let's see how.

Emotional Pricing

In a perfect world, sellers would price their offerings considering reasonable profit margins and realistic sales forecasts. But, like some of the clueless sellers on these shows, many entrepreneurs and small business owners are in love with the product or service they offer and their outrageous prices reflect it. They believe that what they offer is so unique that surely it can command the prices they set. Plus, often what they are selling is really not unique because they haven't done their research homework.

Know the Market and Competition. While setting prices based on competitors can be deadly to small businesses especially, knowing what people are paying for similar or nearly similar products and services can be helpful in setting realistic, realizable prices for the target market demographic.

"Saw It on the Internet" Pricing

These sellers are almost the opposite of the emotional sellers. They've "sort of" done their homework and at least did some searching to see what their item might be worth. But they might be comparing their item with a highly collectible, mint condition version of it. They think their item is as unique as some of the highest priced ones on eBay. Or they might be looking at the selling price or value from a time when the market for it was booming.

Apples to Apples... and then to Oranges. Know how your product or service stacks up to what is currently for sale in the marketplace. Then realize what unique qualities can be capitalized upon.

Sale or Resale?

Inexperienced sellers featured on these shows can also get tripped up by asking for a "retail" price from the shows' stars. They forget that these folks are buying to resell the items. Even funnier is when these sellers try to convince the buyers that they'll "get a lot of money" because the item so unique. Really? The shows' stars deal in these markets all day, every day. They have a good pulse on what's in the marketplace and what's moving.

Know Your Buyer and Why They're Buying. Why is a buyer even considering buying what's for sale? Personal use? Resale? Pricing and selling for the wrong purpose can make a seller appear inexperienced or uninformed, neither of which increase the chances of a sale.

Understand What's Realistic for the Market. Don't set blue sky sales prices based on an offering's erroneously perceived rarity or uniqueness.

Unicorns

Celebrity signatures? Items with historic value? Products that are no longer being made? Unicorns? They all could be very rare. But the big question is: *"Does it have a market?"*

Regardless of how rare or unique an item is, if there are no ready, willing and able buyers for it, the item will not sell, even if it technically has value.

Similarly, small business owners can often get tripped up by trying to offer the most rare and unique product or service on the market. Example: *"We're the only ones making glow-in-the-dark pasta."* Oooookay. Never heard of glow-in-the-dark pasta and don't think we ever will. Yes, it's rare. But a situation where that would be a desirable product is also rare, if not non-existent.

Another point is the difference between rarity and uniqueness. Rarity usually means that there is a limited supply. Uniqueness means that it is different from other offerings. A product or service can be either or both. But rarity and uniqueness do not always equal sale-ability.

Understand the Difference Between Being Unique and Being Marketable. One can sing the *"I'm Unique and/or Rare"* song all day long. But if the market doesn't desire or care about that difference, then sales will be very difficult.

Do Realistic Profit and Loss and Sales Forecasts. Unique and rare products and services may have limited appeal and markets... as well as limited sales. Forecast and budget accordingly.

Chapter 3:
One-Trick Pony

How many products or services should a small business offer? The number will greatly depend on the capacity and resources available. But, unfortunately, some small businesses and entrepreneurs have a single product or product line. Essentially, they're one-trick ponies.

They might do that product or service "trick" well, sometimes very well or too well. They're so good at it, in fact, that they could burn up all the potential sales within a single selling cycle. Many of these may be one-hit wonder sales. Then what happens? These folks may go into an extended sales slump or even be unable to recover and have to go out of business.

But the solution isn't always to expand the number or type of offerings since that can unduly strain the organization and its resources.

Let's look at an example...

Solving the One-Trick Product Puzzle

As many of my followers know, I worked in the promotional products industry for many years. One of the perks of working in this arena is the opportunity to go to the trade shows and see all the new and exciting products.

Every year, there are usually some new companies on the show floor, often showing just one new product in the booth.

At one show some time back, there was a very simple, innovative product that would be an excellent conversation starter at conferences and meetings. But that was the sum and total of what this company was offering. Sadly, I let them scan my badge and their incessant follow-up drove me crazy.

The problem with the product was that it was very conceptual. So it really would require a unique fit between the client and its intended purpose. It was also so innovative that to do the same product at future client events might garner an *"oh, that again"* response. So it had a very narrow band of opportunity making it a one-hit wonder sale for both the product manufacturer and me. But this company is not unique. Many small businesses have the same problem due to limited capacity and resources.

So what can companies with only one or extremely limited product and service selections do?

Add Sales Channels. Seeking out individual customers can be a massive dollar cost, labor and time investment! So consider connecting with retailers, wholesalers, representatives or other distributors who can add a one-off product like this to their portfolio of offerings. With a potentially larger customer base, as well as expanded marketing and distribution capability, this strategy could make sales efforts more efficient. In the example here, the product manufacturer could hook up with a multi-line wholesaler/supplier or manufacturer's representative that works with many promotional product sellers.

Find New Uses. For the example product, it appeared that it could have some retail potential in addition to promotional markets. Sometimes products or services are developed with one target market or application in mind. While that can be good in that it is tailored for the market, there better be enough sales and profit potential within that demographic to make it worthwhile. In evaluating a one-trick offering for other uses, additional costs for advertising, repackaging, additional liability insurance, legal issues, etc. for a different market need to be considered. If the cost is too high to repurpose for some other use, it may not provide enough sales and profit potential, disqualifying new uses as a worthwhile endeavor.

Set Realistic Expectations. If the business really, REALLY wants to offer a one-trick product or service, then they need to set realistic sales goals and expectations for themselves. Demand may not expand! A careful analysis of costs, an achievable sales forecast and a profitable pricing structure are critical to making a go/no go decision for this business or offering.

Be Prepared for the End. The problem with offering only one product is that if the market demand collapses, so can the business, especially if new uses are not developed. All products go through life cycles and could become obsolete, cash cows (we hope!) or may have to change to stay relevant. The end is a good starting point when considering the future potential of a one-trick product or service.

Chapter 4:
Superhero

Had a revelation about my business that can have a profound effect on profitability, productivity and sales. When I was in the promotional product business, I had access to no less than 3,000 different suppliers and over half a million product SKUs. The temptation to use any or all of them was strong, make that STRONG. And here's the scenario that could have gotten me into trouble.

A customer had a "vision" for an upcoming project. I would show him the possibilities that I had as standard offerings through my online shopsites or from my preferred supply chain partners. Um, didn't quite match the unrealistic dream. Then the wild goose chase began!

Database research, calling suppliers, checking catalogs... I could have been putting in hours of work and the sale hadn't even closed yet. Compounding the issue was that a quantity of only 500, maybe even 50, was needed. May sound like a big quantity for a small, solopreneur business. But in the promotional products world, that's usually a small order. Then, after the whole research process, I often got THAT email, the one that said, *"Thanks for your help, but we've decided to [go with another supplier, scrap/postpone the project, not spend the money or some lame excuse]."*

Being concerned about customer service, in the past I would often chase these impossible inquiries (emphasis on "in the past"). But was that really service? Or was I providing these off-the-menu choices out of fear of losing sales and the opportunity to serve?

Then when I got older and wiser, I would send these folks to one of my knowledgeable competitors who could do the project better than I ever could.

Let's look a little deeper at why this type of scenario happens in small businesses...

Like Ford Selling Chevys

Solopreneurs and self-employed folks have to remember the scenario discussed above is like Ford selling Chevys. Ludicrous notion, of course. Except for the sales of used cars of many makes, auto dealers would NEVER entertain the impossible inquiry of a customer who wandered into the dealership asking to buy a new car from a competing manufacturer. Not only would it be detrimental to their brand to offer it, it would cost them more to service this business, too.

Contrast this to small businesses who can be ridiculously prone to taking on impossible projects that are "not in their wheelhouse." If it is so obvious to most bigger businesses, why do the little guys do this?

Fear of Losing Sales. In the early years, especially for consulting or extreme niche offerings, sales can be few and far between. So they latch on to any inquiry that happens to wander in. They end up reinventing the business to meet every single customer demand.

Feeling Like a Superhero... or Want to Appear So. Ever see the contractor trucks that say "Residential, Commercial and Industrial?" Anyone who has a good understanding of the contracting business knows that serving individual consumers is completely different than dealing with commercial and industrial facility managers. A variation on this theme are the consultants who say they work with "small businesses to Fortune 100 clients." Some newbie consultants, particularly those that have come from a corporate background, have an understanding of doing business within large operations. But when they go into business for themselves, they don't feel they have a prayer of getting sales from big businesses (and they may be right). So they take a stab at doing business with individual consumers or other customers out of their comfort and experience zone. Then they get a huge dose of culture shock when they sell in the B2C (business to consumer) and may even give up to go back to a "real job."

Who Are You and Who Are Your Customers? Solopreneurs and consultants who say they serve everybody, don't know who or what they are. Even worse is that they don't know who or what their customers are either. So every inquiry, even the impossible ones, are pursued. They're just hoping that at least some of them will buy.

How to Avoid Doing the Impossible

While networking, you may be the closest thing to what a connection wants or needs. Even though you don't have the ability or capacity to serve them, they reach out to you anyway. Being a friendly networker, you want to help them. But taking on projects or sales that are impossible for you to handle damages your reputation.

Avoiding getting trapped in impossible selling scenarios requires a thorough understanding of your business, its capabilities and limitations:

Nosce Te Ipsum (Know Thyself). Take an inventory of skills, products and services that can be effectively AND cost effectively provided. Be specific to the Nth degree! If the overall skill is marketing, what kind of marketing tasks can be offered? There are probably hundreds of niches to fill in the marketing arena.

Define Customers. Who are those customers that need the products and services that can be offered? Don't say "everybody!" Define the folks by industry, job title, hobbies, age, gender... using several marketing demographic factors helps focus sales and marketing efforts.

Develop a "Menu" of Products and Services... and Stick to It! On the popular restaurant makeover reality shows, one of the common problems plaguing the troubled operations is a bloated menu, sometimes spanning several pages. The inventory, chef skill and marketing of these extensive offerings can cripple the business. But no matter what industry a business is in, all need to develop a "menu" of standard products and services to be offered. This streamlines the operation and focuses marketing and sales efforts. Sticking to this standard menu will turn away some high maintenance customers (see discussions of "off the menu" offerings below). But the meager benefits to be gained from these will almost always not be worth the effort and cost.

Develop a Standard of Service. In addition to the "what" on a menu of products and services, a "how" should also be developed for their delivery. That could mean delivery only by a carrier such as UPS, pickup only in stores, restricting acceptance of orders to online or by phone, limiting sales territory, etc. The cost to deliver goods and services needs to be built into the pricing structure and profit margin projections. **Example:** Some prospects wanted to chat about their promotions with me in their offices. Sorry, folks, that's consulting and it was too expensive for me to chase these types of requests that almost inevitably would result in a measly order of a couple hundred bucks or even one of those "we bought from someone else" emails. (Had it happen too many times!) That's why I developed extensive shopsites they could browse through on their time and dime.

Develop Premium Pricing and Justification for "Off the Menu" Choices. Granted, taking on some impossible projects can help a company stretch its capabilities. But as a daily occurrence, it will drain resources. So if a company wants to offer some "off the menu" products and services, premium higher pricing and/or justification for these offerings needs to be established. **Example #1:** In my previous promotional business, I offered a couple of online shopsites featuring hundreds upon hundreds of different items each. If a customer or prospect could not find a solution within this wide selection, I charged a hefty fee to do a custom search, even if the sale did not close. Often that ended the discussion OR they discovered a standard offering that would suffice. This weeded out the tire kickers. **Example #2:** I received an inquiry to do promotions for a television show. While I didn't charge premium prices, I did justify accepting it with the goal of learning about the "off MY menu" entertainment industry to see if it was worth pursuing in the future. It wasn't and I was glad for the lesson this job provided.

Refer Impossible Business to Appropriate Competitors and Allied Businesses. Developing a network of friendly and competent competitors and allied businesses is also key to eliminating doing impossible business. As soon as an inquiry that doesn't meet the standard customer profile is received, it should be evaluated for referral to other networking colleagues that could handle it more appropriately. You as the referring business also win by looking like a well-connected and knowledgeable businessperson.

Chapter 5:
The Accidental Charity

While many companies get involved in making donations to charitable or community causes, small businesses that do are at a higher risk since the dollar or time outlay can represent a greater share of the budget than for larger organizations. On the flip side, small businesses may heavily rely on bartered, donated or free products and services, and act as a receiving "charity" of sorts. Let's look at both sides of this equation...

Doing Good or Doing Business?
Since the corporate social responsibility (CSR) trend became popular, companies of all sizes seem to want to add a "giving back" component to their businesses. Some are doing it to satisfy the altruistic motives of their owners, leaders, shareholders or customers. Others are seeking to put their companies in a market leadership position by marketing their socially responsible initiatives alongside their products and services (meta message: *"We do good. You should buy from us."*).

Overall, this is considered to be positive. However, what can happen, particularly on the small business level, is letting these CSR initiatives overtake financial initiatives. Acting like a charity that has deep pockets will eventually take its toll and negatively impact a small business' resources.

Why does this happen?

Owners are Too Emotionally Invested in the Cause. This happens particularly in cases where the small business owner has been personally impacted. For example, an owner who survived cancer may want to donate to cancer support or research causes, regardless of whether it makes sense for the company's audience, brand or budget.

It Aligns with the Zeitgeist or Audience, but Not with the Company or its Values. In this instance, a company may choose to support a cause that's "hot" at the moment or one that their communities think is important. However, it may not align with the company's values or operations. For example, when "green" initiatives were hot, companies wanted to jump on board with causes that saved the environment, even if they themselves didn't follow green practices. This is a huge integrity lapse.

Owners Overestimate the Impact of Their CSR Initiatives. When small business owners are passionately dedicated to a cause, they want to change the world! Unless their company is of adequate size to invest significant sums of money or other resources, small business CSR initiatives will usually amount to only small to moderate donations. Because of their limited ability to give, they can feel they're not doing enough to "change the world" and may overcommit in terms of either financial or time donations.

Owners and Donation Recipients Underestimate the Cost of CSR Initiatives. Charities and associations sometimes approach small service businesses with requests for donations of time, as well as money. When it comes to time, donation requesters figure that it doesn't cost the small business any hard dollars. Sadly, small businesses often feel the same way! This is an exceptionally slippery slope. The charities can easily come to expect these free services, even to the point of building them into their budget framework. On the giving side, the small service businesses feel that what they offer is "free" and can underestimate the demands these time and talent donations will entail.

Acting Like a Charity

Relying on donated, bartered or free services and products to operate can be helpful to a small business. However, if a significant portion of the operation or mission critical business expenses are funded in this manner, the business has, in essence, become a charity who relies on the kindness of others.

What happens when those products and services, or those that provide them, disappear? The business then can be faced with huge costs and may not even be able to operate for very long, if at all.

Why does this happen?

Owner Has Friends Who Want Something. Those who donate to or barter with a small business have their own goals. They're not doing it solely out of the goodness of their hearts. These people want something! Owners sometimes mistake these relationships as kindness and get hurt when these relationships go sour, dissolve or their "donors" become demanding.

Owner is Undercapitalized and Needs Help. If an owner is not properly capitalized to open or operate a small business, he may become dependent on bartered, free or donated goods and services. Unfortunately, this only masks a precarious financial situation.

Avoiding the Small Business-Acting-Like-Charity Trap

Avoiding the mental, emotional and financial trap of acting like a charity takes discipline! Here are some tips for refraining from charity-like behavior:

Evaluate the Value of Any Donation to Causes. Assess what any donation will do for the business. If it cannot be tied to one of the company's values or goals, reconsider. Do a pros and cons list if necessary. If it doesn't align with the business' objectives, consider making personal—not business—donations.

Add It Up. Sometimes the donations requested from small businesses are small. But cumulatively, they can add up. Ten dollars here, twenty-five there. Miscellaneous small dollar amounts can add up to hundreds, even thousands, of dollars of a business' budget per year. Granted, it may be tax deductible (check with your CPA or tax advisor). Even considering tax write-off advantages, cash flow is still king.

Scrutinize Every Barter Agreement. When a friend suggests a barter agreement, it's easy to slip into agreeing to it based on the relationship value, not the values being exchanged. Carefully assess the realistic value being provided by both parties and **GET IT IN WRITING!** Also, barter agreements can have tax ramifications. Consult a CPA and an attorney for details on creating and managing these agreements.

Do a Profit and Loss "As If" Analysis. Add the dollar value in freebies or bartered benefits the business receives into a hypothetical profit and loss calculation "as if" they were paid. This will provide some perspective on the real costs of doing business. While it will likely show that these benefits have a positive impact on the bottom line by accepting them, imagine if these benefits were to suddenly disappear. How would these items be paid with cash? Could they be even be paid? Also remember, as noted above, that barter arrangements could have tax ramifications.

BOUNDARY BLUNDERS

Chapter 6:
Bandwidth Bandits

The Bandwidth Problem

7:30 a.m. I wander into the convention center meeting room to check on tech setups and connections, including Wi-Fi for the Internet, to show some video examples during a conference session on marketing videos I would be presenting at 11:00 a.m. All good.

11:00 a.m. The Wi-Fi bandwidth has been exceeded for the convention center. I have zero connectivity to the Internet. My session collapsed in an instant and I had to ad lib for an hour. What a speaking nightmare!

For the next sessions in another city, the conference education coordinator and I decided that we'd devise presentations that didn't require Wi-Fi. Everything went smoother the next time.

Besides the lessons for public speaking and events, this story illustrates the problem of bandwidth—also known as capacity limitations—in business. And it's not just for technology. Like my 7:30 a.m. soundcheck before the swarms of attendees arrived, everything works perfectly when there are only a few customers. Then when growth occurs—blam!—system fail.

This issue can be particularly difficult for small business owners and entrepreneurs, even though it can signal a good problem to have... growth. In other cases, newbie businesses can completely underestimate their staffing, cash and resource bandwidth before they even open their doors. Then they are playing catch up from the moment they open up.

The Problem of Scale and The Crafter Fantasy

I've enjoyed doing needlework off and on since I was about nine years old. Every once in a while over the years, I'll get bit by the *"Could I make a living (or part of it) doing this?"* bug. Then my business self gets a grip and "The Crafter Fantasy" is over instantly. Why?

While I enjoy these pursuits, there is no way I have the capacity (or talent) to make more than a few projects a week. Considering the market pricing, sales demand, administrative costs and profit margins I would need to make this a worthwhile pursuit, this fantasy cannot become reality.

The situation illustrates the capacity problem of a business that does not scale without significant investment. It's one that many crafters, artists and passion-based entrepreneurs fall into. They love what they do, but their "art" can take a long time to complete. Scaling up operations to keep up with demand is almost impossible without hiring labor (since working faster and longer is not an option) or investing in equipment to automate operations (which could destroy the "art" part).

The flip side is that these capacity limitations also limit how much money can be made. If a small business only has the bandwidth to complete one to a few projects per week, then those projects better be high paying ones to enable them to pay their bills... and themselves.

How Dog Pee Affects My Company's Bandwidth

Sometimes capacity limitations in a small business can be caused by forces other than those in the business. Care of children, parents, relatives, spouses or even pets can limit the time and energy bandwidth of a small business owner.

At my house, one of my dogs has bladder issues that come and go throughout the year as the seasons change. Worst part is that she often falls asleep and doesn't realize she needs to pee. So I have to be pretty diligent about making sure she's outside several times a day.

Using doggie diapers would be challenging since she and her dog pal would "repurpose" them as toys. Plus, she's never been crated after she reached adult age and wants to be with her dog buddy. Crating would cause her additional stress and anxiety since her problem is not behavioral, it's physical.

Since other than this issue, she's a healthy dog, I just have to be diligent about letting her out every few hours. As you can imagine, this puts me on a virtual "leash," limiting time away from home to a few hours unless I have another caregiver available. But hiring petsitters on a continuing basis can get pricey over time.

What to do? Schedule the care AND business hours! Similar to my email management system, I keep regular business hours during the work week, working in a dog care routine that helps preserve my precious bandwidth while preventing additional work from dog accidents.

Assessing and Dealing with Capacity Limitations

Here are some additional thoughts on learning to deal with the capacity limitations that plague many operations, especially small businesses and entrepreneurial ventures:

Do a Time Study. Regardless of whether it is craft, service or product based, do a time study on how long it takes to create, sell and service what the company offers. (See a later chapter for a discussion on doing a time study.)

Forecast Sales as Accurately as Possible. Forecasting sales and demand, especially in a new or expanding business can be tricky. However, without it, it is impossible to plan for capacity needs.

Control Advertising to Help Control Demand. Investing in a big advertising spend might create a good deal of traffic and sales. That is usually a good thing. However, if the business does not have the capacity to handle the load, it will result in poor customer service and unhappy customers. Start with a smaller, realistic advertising rollout.

Communicate the Limitations. Most small business people don't want to admit that they are incapable of handling any and all sales that come their way. But being honest with customers about limitations can help reduce customer complaints.

Limit Offerings. This helps solve the "trying to be everything to everyone" problem. Restaurants are often guilty of offering too large a menu that is impossible to sustain on all operational levels. Whether in the restaurant business or not, limit the "menu" of products and services to only those for which the company has capacity and competitive advantage.

Consider Alternative Offerings that Do Scale. If a company has a limited product or service portfolio to offer—even a one-trick pony as we discussed earlier—seeking out alternative streams of income that can scale for minimal investment can help keep the company doing what it loves while still building its brand. Going back to my crafter fantasy, instead of just offering completed works, I could begin designing, publishing and selling original patterns or instruction materials. Especially if these are offered electronically or as a print-on-demand basis, there is less chance of running into capacity or inventory issues.

Chapter 7:
Time Thieves

Do you know—really know!—how much time it takes you—yes, you specifically—to do any task at home or work? Sadly, many people don't have a clue how much time it takes to do the myriad of tasks on their over-multitasked agendas. And the time required can vary widely from person to person.

Here's the challenge. Take the time (pun intended) to track the time spent on every single little activity for a week or a month (even better since some weeks have varied activities). Include the business and personal. Sleeping, eating, email, social media, reading, exercising, family time, personal and health care, watching TV... don't cheat, include it all, okay?

Surprised at what you found? I'm sure you are, just as I was.

Let's get one thing clear. There is no right or wrong expenditure of time, just more or less effective use of the minutes and hours of our limited lifespans.

It's Been a Long Time

Looking at your time logs, did you notice that you spend an inordinate amount of time doing certain activities compared to others? See if any of these apply:

- Don't really know how to do the activity, so it takes so much longer.
- You feel obligated to do it.
- It helps you avoid doing other things you don't like.
- You feel like you're doing something even if it's busywork.
- You don't know what else to do.
- Force of habit.

If you could agree with any of the above, it's time to take a deeper look at what you're doing with your time and your life. Some activities might be better accomplished by delegating or eliminating them or finding a better way to do them.

But avoid the temptation to increase multitasking to accomplish everything! This can lead to stress and, ironically, accomplishing less due to lack of focus.

How Many Work Weeks Does that Take?

Looking at my time log a few years back, I realized that I was spending on the order of 3 to 4 hours (or more) every day (sometimes on weekends, too) on social media. Let's multiply that out, using 3 hours on average. And because I was most concerned about its effect on my working time, let's just consider the five weekdays.

3 hours per day on social media X 5 weekdays = 15 hours per week

15 hours per week ÷ 40 hours in a standard work week = 37.5% of work week spent on social media

37.5% X 52 weeks per year = 19.5 work weeks spent on this activity annually

Yowsa! What was I doing? What did I have to show for this investment? And what was I going to do to get this under control?

My solution? Schedule it! Now I only spend 30 minutes a day maximum on social media for each weekday, with weekends off. Here is my revised investment:

0.5 hours per day on social media X 5 weekdays = 2.5 hours per week

2.5 hours per week ÷ 40 hours in a standard work week = 6.25% of work week spent on social media

6.25% X 52 weeks per year = 3.25 work weeks spent on this activity annually

That's better!

So how many work weeks does it take you for various tasks? Here are the formulas:

Formula 1: *Number of hours per day on average X Number of weekdays spent on the activity = Number of hours spent doing the activity per week*

Formula 2: *Number of hours spent doing the activity per week ÷ 40 hours in a standard work week = Percentage of work week dedicated to this activity*

Formula 3: *Percentage of work week dedicated to this activity X Number of weeks in a year = Number of work weeks spent annually in this activity*

Even worse is when you multiply those hours by your hourly income rate. Try this for the hours spent on email and social media. No, neither one is free! Be prepared to be shocked to learn how much your activities "cost" you.

Chapter 8:
Cold Pizza

During challenging economic times and sales slumps, small business owners often are tempted to venture quite far from their offices or homes in search of sales. Ironically, in good economic times, sales in far flung regions are also often pursued. The reasoning in that case is that the sales are there, go get 'em while the getting is good. Unfortunately, regardless of the motivation, spanning a sales territory beyond what is effective can destroy profit margins while building sales.

On the opposite end of the sales spectrum, reducing a sales territory to too small a region may reduce sales volumes to the point of not being able provide enough revenues to sustain a business.

Striking the right balance when setting and managing a territory is one of the most important sales techniques to master to sustain and grow revenues.

How Far Should Your Sales Territory Span? (The Cold Pizza Issue.)

Technically, no sale is impossible if dollars, time and legal restrictions are not factors. But in the real world of money and manpower, many sales are impractical or improbable.

There are actually two major considerations when setting the boundaries of a territory:

1. At what point does it become unprofitable to provide acceptable customer service?

2. What number of calls will need to be made within a specified reporting period (week, month, quarter or whatever time period is relevant) to achieve sales revenue goals? At what distance does it become impossible to achieve that call volume within that time frame?

Both of these considerations require diligent tracking of costs, profit margins, sales and service activities. In the first year of a business, territory setting may include some trial and error. But after the first full fiscal year, enough data should be available to begin refining territories. This refining and review process should be done at least annually as changes occur in the business and marketplace.

As discussed in a previous chapter, you may wish to do a time study to see exactly how much time in work weeks you are spending in commuting to AND from various business or networking opportunities. When I did this, I realized how much time I was spending on networking events and clients way out of my area... and how little I was gaining from them since I couldn't adequately service these areas either.

Example: Pizza restaurants typically restrict their delivery zones (their sales territories) to within a few miles of their location. Why? Because beyond that point, delivery times can take too long, resulting in angry customers and cold pizza!

Clustering Sales Calls

One of the easiest ways to optimize sales territories is to cluster sales and service calls. Plan to spend a morning, afternoon or day making calls on customers that are physically near each other. This obviously reduces the time necessary to meet several customers. But it also reduces travel costs for gasoline, vehicle wear, airfare, taxi fares, etc.

Essentially, these calls become a route. If a target customer doesn't happen to be available on the day scheduled for the remainder of the calls, that customer can be visited on the next scheduled route to that area. Do not make special calls to these prospects on other days unless it will result in a guaranteed big score! Making exceptions derails the route for other days.

Many salespeople, managers and owners may be worried that they will appear as not being service oriented and may lose sales. The survival or success of the business never likely hinges on just one sale… and it shouldn't! As well, customers who demand or expect "drop everything" attention may be high maintenance on the customer service side of the sale and be unprofitable in the long run.

Should a Low Performing Sales Territory be Dropped?

What if after best efforts, a sales territory is in a slump? Should that region be dropped? Maybe, maybe not.

Determine if these factors may be the culprit:

Changes in the Market. If the area has performed well in the past, evaluate if some changes are occurring in the territory. Do those changes represent a temporary or permanent change in demographic makeup or market demand? If a permanent shift, dropping or limiting service to the region should be considered.

Sales Issues. Are you (or your sales representative) equipped to handle these customers? Is it too demanding? Does it require multiple sales calls? Frequent review of sales results can help determine if staffing changes or additions need to be made to revive an underperforming region.

Limiting the Unlimited Territory of the Internet

The Internet has opened up the entire world as potential customers. Even though this presents the possibility of almost unlimited territories for sales, businesses still need to restrict their service areas due to a variety of logistical factors.

The first and most obvious factor limiting Internet sales territories is the physical movement of products. Not only can freight be prohibitively expensive, but customs and taxation issues can balloon the cost of international sales even further. Compounding the issue are commerce and product safety laws that vary from country to country, usually requiring legal counsel. Topping off the troubles are currency exchange rates which can destroy profit margins if sales are not priced properly.

While international sales are not impossible and can be very lucrative for some markets, a thorough cost versus benefit analysis should be done before attempting these sales. Stray Internet inquiries from international markets are not worth pursuing and, if possible, should be referred to friendly competitors who are in or frequently serve that country.

Some services and digital products do offer international sales possibilities if handled properly. For example, those who self-publish on Amazon's Kindle Direct Program have the opportunity to sell their works on the international stage and Amazon handles all the currency and commerce details.

Chapter 9:
"I Can Also Do That"

Was commiserating with a fellow marketing professional about how we take on projects that are unprofitable and unsatisfying, often as favors to loyal clients or friends. *"Why do we do that?"* we asked ourselves. We both concluded that we're suffering from the *"I Can Also Do That"* problem with our marketing strategies.

Symptoms of the *"I Can Also Do That"* Problem

The *"I Can Also Do That"* problem can exhibit itself in a variety of ways:

The Never Ending "We Do" List. A small business website listing every possible product or service that could (emphasis on "could") be provided by the business is the tell-tale sign. Surely, a potential customer has got to find something they want in this list, right? For example, a small business that offers marketing services lists that they do website design, graphic design, direct mail, SEO, copywriting, public relations, mobile marketing, promotional products... the list goes on and on. Having competency in all of those areas would be a trick for even a large company!

Clinging to Corporate. Many small business owners and freelance micro businesses are "refugees" from the corporate world. In that former life, they may have done a wide variety of projects and tasks, all under the banner (and budget!) of their corporate home. So their assessment of the true costs of doing a buffet of projects is skewed and unrealistic. They might know the mechanics of getting any of these projects done. But should they actually take this work on? Probably not since it might be way beyond their capabilities, both financially and logistically.

Multiple Business Cards. *"Here's my card for my such-and-such business and here's my card for my other business."* This situation is often encountered at networking events. One has to ask, *"So, which business are you really in?"* In many cases, this happens when small business folks take on another opportunity and cannot mix the two businesses, either due to legal or other restrictions or it just doesn't fit well with the other work they do.

Unusual Increases in COGS and Overhead Costs. Taking on work that is not ideal for the business can often be very costly in terms of both time and hard dollar costs. If cost of goods sold (COGS) and overhead expenses are increasing out of control, taking on work that is unprofitable might be the culprit. Regularly monitoring profit margins and pricing strategies can bring these issues to light.

The Fear Behind It All

One of the greatest reasons why otherwise smart marketers and small businesses take on less-than-ideal work and pursue conflicted marketing strategies stems from fears of loss:

Loss of Clients. At some level, they feel that if they stand up to loyal clients and tell them that they cannot or will not take on a particular project, they'll lose those clients. They feel that unless they go above and beyond what is realistically possible, they'll be seen as providing poor customer service.

Loss of Opportunities. Similar to the fear of losing current clients, they fear that they'll miss out on opportunities for new sales if they don't take on some not-so-ideal work.

Loss of Cash Flow. When economic times get tough, it's all the more tempting to take on work that is inappropriate to make ends meet.

Unfortunately, what happens in all of these scenarios is that this unfit work takes up the time and energy needed to find and service ideal clients and projects.

Avoiding the Marketing Strategy Mashup and Mismatch

Avoiding the mashup and mismatch of conflicting marketing strategies and target markets is done in two simple (but often not easy!) ways:

Focus! Self-doubt over being able to find enough appropriate clients and work causes small business owners to chase everything that even looks like a lead. Be absolutely clear on what constitutes an ideal customer or project.

Just Say No. It is essential to learn to say no to free up time, resources and energy to pursue only ideal opportunities.

Chapter 10:
Too Many Choices

All or Nothing

After a lovely lunch at a French bakery and restaurant, my neighbor friend and I walked across the street to a tea shop to grab a beverage for the drive home. What a darling place this was! Daintily and whimsically decorated and selling almost every imaginable tea and tea gadget. But that was the problem.

Walked up to the tea bar and asked for an iced green tea (a daily routine for me). The barista pointed out my options on an overhead board that was maybe 10 feet by 4 feet, literally covered with lists of teas available. There might have been up to 60 varieties or more, some choices having "guess what this is" type names. After getting dizzy from staring at the list for a number of minutes, I randomly chose a peach version that was okay, but not something I'd order again. Definitely not something I'd make a special trip to get.

The Problems Caused by Marketing Too Many Choices

We always want choice because we want to feel like we're in control. But when presented with too many choices, we have difficulty processing our options and may be disappointed with any choice we make... or worse, choose nothing at all due to overwhelm, as evidenced by the above example. Translation: Less sales.

Offering too many choices is an exceptionally critical problem for small businesses, solopreneurs and consultants. In addition to driving away or lowering sales by overwhelming their customers, they overwhelm their expenses, too, by offering too many options. Added inventory, more warehousing, additional staffing, more marketing costs... the stresses that too many choices can add to a smaller operation are legion.

The "Good, Better, Best" Strategy

Three is a magical and mystical number in many cultures. But it can also be a winner in marketing since it can make it easier for customers to make a decision from this limited set of options.

Offering three levels of choice was made popular by retailing pioneers such as Sears and Montgomery Ward in their heyday. A "Good, Better, Best" range of options was common in their catalogs and in stores.

This range of options is common in many other arenas, too, particularly for services. Many online services today offer an entry-level "freemium" service (the "good"), with upgrades to standard (the "better") and premium (the "best") paid service levels. This set of options usually isn't decided upon by chance, it's by design.

Back to the Tea Shop...

In many everyday product and service marketing scenarios, a "Good, Better, Best" or limited-tier offering structure is practical for both businesses and customers. But can a case be made for offering everything imaginable such as the tea shop did? Yes, with some qualifications.

Some markets are what I would call "connoisseur" markets. In these cases, customers are highly educated on the subtle nuances between product or service offerings. They are looking for the unique, the rare, the elite, the best, the limited edition. Examples would include *art, antiques, wine, comic books, collectibles, luxury items, specialty food items*, etc. Widely available offerings can be considered pedestrian. So these discriminating customers want choice—even many choices!—because they can easily discern value. The hunt for the most valuable is a game.

As well, a *mass customization* trend has been evolving. Enabled by technology, manufacturers and service providers can allow their customers to pick and choose from a list of product and feature combinations to suit their needs, the result being a totally one-off product or service. For example, athletic shoes can now be ordered with the customer's unique choice of color and fabric combinations.

Mass customization is a hybrid of marketing strategies when it comes to choice. In some cases, the sheer number of unique feature combinations a customer can order may run into the hundreds or thousands! Yet, the manufactured inventory is kept low because the order is only created on demand. Plus, the range of features that can be selected is often limited, making it more cost-effective for the business and narrowing the field (at least to some degree) for the customer.

With the advent of on-demand and 3D printing technology, this trend can be expected to grow... and offer customers choices beyond their current imagining. But then will we run into the same old "too many choices" problem?

How to Choose Your Choices

So how do you choose what choices to offer your customers? Your choice in choices will depend on:

Type of Customer. Are your customers connoisseurs of what you offer who may want a lot of choice? Don't automatically say yes! If you ask customers if they want many choices, they will likely say they do, even if they don't really need or want that much field of choice. Research your market's demographics, psychographics and buying behaviors to home in on what choice scenario makes them tick... and buy. You might be surprised at how many customers are looking for you to lead them through a logical and limited choice funnel. Once I limited my own service offerings, and was very clear about those choices in my marketing, I found that the referrals and inquiries I got were higher quality and lower investment for my business.

Capacity Limitations. Mass customization and large, varied inventories can usually only be pursued by organizations that have sufficient resources in terms of facilities, time, staffing and money. Be realistic about your limitations!

Chapter 11:
Muddled Streams of Income

Diversification can be key to creating a sustainable business for an organization of any size, including a small business. This is sometimes referred to as "multiple streams of income." As with any other business strategy, multiple income stream strategies have pros and cons that need to seriously be considered.

What are Multiple Streams of Income?
Multiple streams of income can sometimes be referred to as "profit centers" if the income comes into and through the same business. Essentially, these streams then operate as different product or service areas, all operating under one company umbrella. **Example:** In my business, I have four distinct streams of income: 1) Self publishing and marketing coaching; 2) Public speaking; 3) Book sales; and, 4) Writing services. Yet, I have not set up four separate companies.

In other cases, streams are completely separate businesses or investments, all owned (either in whole or in part) by one organization or individual.

Pros

The strongest reason for using a multiple streams of income business strategy is that when one part of the business hits a sales slump or is seasonally slow, these secondary revenue sources can help make up for the loss. This can create a steadier income picture through the year and may help avoid borrowing for regularly occurring expenses such as labor, utilities and rent.

In addition to seasonal or temporary fluctuations in income, these strategies can help keep a business in business should one or more of the profit centers completely dry up due to economic, consumer preference and technological changes.

Sometimes growth or expansion into new markets can drain resources, too. Keeping the business afloat with multiple or secondary profit centers can help propel the overall organization to new success.

As well, investing in profit centers that are similar to or relate to the primary business can provide economies of scale and synergies that capitalize on the company's strengths and access to customer bases.

Cons

While having the safety net of additional income sources can help sustain or build a business, it can also kill a business quickly if one or more of these centers cause too much of a drag on overall resources. This can create a "Robbing Peter to Pay Paul" scenario. If only overall revenues are considered when evaluating financial results, this situation is more likely to occur, masking individual revenue stream troubles.

Monitoring multiple revenue streams can be time consuming and confusing if effective and efficient systems are not set up for reporting. **Example:** When I was selling promotional products as one of my additional income streams, I needed the help of an outside bookkeeper to set up special reports in my accounting software package to properly evaluate revenues, expenses and profits. This took some time and expense because one of the businesses is retail based, required sales tax reporting and had a separate ecommerce system that didn't integrate with the accounting software. Even with that help, it still required some more complicated Excel spreadsheets to get the insight I wanted.

From a marketing perspective, multiple offerings can confuse a company's core message and branding, leading customers to question, *"So who and what are you today?"*

Real Life Example: Muddled Streams of Income

Several years ago, being "green" was all the rage. And I jumped on that wagon almost instantly by offering more ecofriendly promotional products. I believed in the greener business agenda and it helped build my status as a green marketing expert which was great.

But it also drew a lot of people to me that wanted me to represent their "green" consumer products, reasoning that I already had an established network who knew, liked and trusted me and would be interested in what I have to say. In theory, that sounded like a good idea since it aligned with my personal and professional values. Key phrase here is "in theory." It was a disaster, resulting in losing clients, losing focus and some money, too. It wasn't an income stream; it was a slurry!

What was wrong with this multiple stream of income plan? Because I sold to the B2B (business to business) market, selling B2C (business to consumer) goods was a horrendous fit. Even though I have many personal friendships with clients, they weren't exactly thrilled about discussing a greener consumer product with me. It made my sales conversations chaotic and even uncomfortable. Adding to the mess was that many of my clients had mixed feelings about greener initiatives.

Wish I could say that was the only instance where I tried the B2B plus B2C mixture, but it wasn't. And every time I wandered into this mismatch of markets, I was reminded why I shouldn't do it.

Luckily, I've learned my lesson over the years and strongly scrutinize every additional income opportunity.

Tips for Using Multiple Streams of Income More Successfully

Choose Logical Additional Income Streams and Profit Centers. Sure, mega entrepreneurs such as Virgin's Richard Branson can invest in profit centers and businesses as diverse as music to space travel. But it is unlikely that most small business owners are in that elite group. Choose opportunities that provide economies of scale and synergies between income streams to capitalize on assets and strengths.

Run Separate Financial Reports for Each Profit Center or Business. To avoid the "Robbing Peter to Pay Paul" scenario, run separate financial reports for each stream of income. Direct expenses and COGS (Cost of Goods Sold) for that stream need to be included. Also, each stream should "contribute" to overhead for the entire operation to avoid having one stream drag the organization into an unprofitable state. Consult a CPA or bookkeeping professional to determine contribution percentages for each center.

Decide on Acceptable Limits for One Profit Center's Drag on Overall Finances. Especially when using multiple streams of income to fuel new growth or get through a rough patch, a point where the high investment opportunity's drag on the overall financial health becomes unacceptable needs to be established. When getting close to that point, it is a warning sign that action and decisions must be taken to keep financially healthy.

Chapter 12:
When Clients are Friends

The Toughest Jobs You'll Ever Get

One of the best things about being in business for yourself is the opportunity to create new friendships within your network. But when those "friends" decide to become clients, these relationships enter a whole new, challenging dimension.

Drawing the line between what is friendly conversation and what is business can be tricky. Brain picking or *"I just have a quick question"* requests can back a small business owner (especially consultants!) into a corner. Accommodate the request, forfeit the fee and save the friendship? Or stand firm, charge and possibly jeopardize the friendship and the sale?

Why I Might Not Want Coffee With You

It's no secret that I love hanging with friends at popular coffee shops. But that's also where I can get myself into trouble when I meet with business friends.

The atmosphere is friendly and the conversation easily meanders from family and fun to business. Then a *"What should I do about...?"* question enters the exchange. This is a little like a brain picking bonus round. This is consultation without compensation.

Best defense is to be prepared for the "coffee consult" request. Kindly suggest that the topic would be better addressed in an official engagement.

Sign Off or Sign Out!

If a friend is amenable to officially doing business with you, you may be tempted to dispense with some of your normal procedures and paperwork. DON'T! Always get a sign off from your friend on whatever paperwork you do with non-friend clients. If things ever go awry while working together, you'll be glad you did.

Keeping Friends Accountable

Another tough aspect when clients are friends is holding them accountable for payments, performance and deadlines.

As friends, you may be aware of some financial challenges your client friend is facing. So it may be tempting to be flexible on payment due dates or forego any prepayment requirements. Beware of these situations:

Services easily lose their value once rendered. Clients who are financially challenged can sometimes slip into *"Well, I don't think it was worth that"* mode when an invoice arrives. A prepayment policy can help prevent some of these situations.

Pay to play. If you're aware of a client friend's financial difficulties, be honest about your expectations for payment for what you are offering. Again, a prepayment policy might help your friend become both financially and emotionally invested into working with you... or it will give them a reality check.

Discounting dangers. If you feel inclined to offer a friend discount (hint: a discount is never required!), make sure that all invoicing clearly shows the regular price and that it was discounted, as well as why it was discounted. The danger in discounting is that your friend could mentally peg the value and price of your products and services to be at the discounted rate from here to forevermore, not to mention that she may tell her friends what she actually paid. Then your client friend's friends may be expecting that rate, too. When discounting your services, you yourself may also slip into thinking that you won't provide your standard level of service or products to make up for the lower payment. Don't automatically discount for friends without considering the consequences.

Setting boundaries. If your client has had friend-level anytime cell phone, email and texting access to you, you may need to set some boundaries and procedures on access during your work together. Be clear about what will and will not be allowed. If you do wish to continue to have regular "friendly" chatter, then be very careful to call out when the connection veers into business territory. If not, you may find that you'll be giving away hours of unpaid consulting or service time.

Setting expectations for performance and deadlines and, more importantly, sticking to them, can be challenging with friends. Sometimes addressing payment for products and services helps put client friends into work mode since they don't want to waste their investment. But you may still experience some friend backsliding in terms of meeting deadlines and accomplishing tasks. Be honest about performance and progress throughout the engagement.

Bartering Boundaries

Another difficult, but related scenario, comes up when a friend asks to "barter" for your products or services. Sometimes this can be a win-win for both parties. On other occasions, it can be disastrous, especially if the bartered products or services from the friend are something you don't really need or want... or, worse, something you'd rather purchase from someone else other than your friend.

While it may be difficult to tell your friend when a barter is not an ideal fit for you, it's usually better than becoming resentful about providing products or services for less than you feel you're worth.

Don't forget to go through your usual procedures and paperwork for bartered services. **Get it in writing!** As well, bartering can carry tax ramifications. Consult with your CPA or accounting professional on bartering tax rules that will apply to you.

Don't "Friend" Out On Your Responsibilities Either!

In addition to friends expecting unpaid perks and privileges, small business folks can also easily slip into thinking that "it's just a friend" mode and not provide the same high level of service that they offer to regular customers.

Just as clients can be more invested into an official business relationship when they pay, when you get properly compensated for what you offer, you'll also be more inclined to do your best.

Chapter 13:
The Price is Wrong

Next to forecasting sales, setting pricing strategies in marketing a product or service is one of the toughest jobs facing small business owners. And many get it wrong.

Competitive Pricing Models: Why You Can't Compete with Giants

Matching what competitors are offering as prices is a strategy often pursued by larger organizations and retailers who can absorb some losses from offering less than profitable pricing, usually to gain higher market share. Products and services offered at these rock bottom prices are referred to as loss leaders. This strategy banks on the hope that customers will make additional purchases at retail or above OR make aftermarket purchases in the future. **Example:** Ink jet printers are offered at super low prices so that the manufacturer can make money on the printing cartridges in the future.

Businesses who use competitive pricing strategies carefully watch what their nearest competitors are offering for the identical (or very similar) offerings, adjusting pricing to either match or come close to that of others. The key phrase here is "identical (or very similar) offerings." If the business is a large enough retailer (such as Walmart or Target), continuous pricing adjustments of this type require significant technology and administrative investments which are usually out of the range of small businesses.

While it is important for businesses of all sizes and types to have knowledge of prices in their marketplace, competitive pricing can be one of the most financially dangerous pricing models for small businesses. Totally basing prices on competitors can kill a business' profits even to the point of going out of business. So this strategy is usually pursued by large companies that have a large array of products and services to offer which can offset losses from discounting or price matching.

But how does competitive pricing work in small businesses? Some real life examples should illustrate.

When the Same Thing is NOT the Same Thing. When I sold promotional products, newer and less experienced customers were usually sticker-shocked at how much an item cost when purchased for promotional purposes. *"But I can get a Hanes T shirt at Target for $3!"* they mused when I would quote a price of $6 (or more) for what they felt was the same shirt with just some printing on it. In some cases it was the same shirt or something very similar.

Here's why my prices were higher. Large retailers are buying product by the truckloads. Notice that it is truckloads with a "s." They have huge centralized buying forces that negotiate based on volume and many other factors such as shipping. A 144-shirt order was a short, special order run for my suppliers and even for a small distributor like myself. Plus, these small, uninformed customers were buying occasionally and I didn't know when their next order might come in. Additionally, my suppliers and I incurred costs to set up and process these small, one-off orders, costs which were also built into my quoted price. Thus I had to quote higher pricing to cover my costs to handhold them for a small order without guarantees for future business. **Lesson:** If you're a one-person business, you cannot compete with mega retailers (offline or online) on price. As well, you are probably offering a customized or personalized version of whatever product or service the customer is buying. It's a proverbial apples to oranges comparison!

Bully Buyers. I also dealt with some bully buyers. They were used to grinding down their vendors, some of whom were my much larger competitors. Had one particularly large customer who bluntly told me that I would have to lower my prices on promotional golf balls for their upcoming outing. For those of you who understand golf retailing, the margins can be razor thin. If I did lower my prices, I would have been paying to do the order. I passed on that opportunity. **Lesson:** Know your limits and when to walk away. Also know who your genuine direct competitors are. Again, make sure it's apples to apples in terms of both what's offered and who's offering it.

All Business is NOT Good Business. I worked with an organization that had a "all business is good business" mindset. This group would cut prices and match services to whatever the competition (large or small) was giving just because they felt that any money coming in was good... even if the work was unprofitable. Unfortunately, when I went into business for myself, I blindly adopted the same philosophy. It had a huge negative impact on my business until I got wise and changed my behavior. **Lesson:** Learn to read your financial statements! Knowing what it costs you to stay in business will help you stay in business… and set boundaries for what you will and will not accept in terms of business opportunities.

Value-Based Pricing Models

How should prices be set for services, particularly unique services and custom projects? This is one of the toughest pricing scenarios because it is not usually based on costs, but on the value of knowledge, experience and expertise.

Using competitive pricing can be a slippery slope toward becoming unprofitable in custom service businesses. For example, good writers can be paid very handsomely for their skills. However, low cost content sites online can offer written content for only a few dollars per project. Competent writers who lower their prices to compete with these sites devalue their expertise and quickly become frustrated or financially strapped.

But the question remains as to how to price services based on value. The following are some strategies that consultants and other service providers may use as a starting point for setting service pricing:

Employment Equivalent. Some professionals who make the leap from employment to offering their expertise as consultants on the open market use their employment salary as a basis for what to charge customers. For example, an annual salary could be divided by an annual number of hours based on a standard 40-hour work week (52 weeks X 40 hours = 2,080 annual hours). This could work if services are sold to clients similar to those of the previous employer. If no similar employment history is available, looking at industry reports for salaries in similar professions can also provide a baseline hourly rate. The caution is that it may not properly cover the expenses of offering these services as a business. So a thorough evaluation of expenses needs to be done prior to setting an hourly consulting rate. Consult a CPA or accounting professional if unsure of how to do this.

Custom Project Quoting. Many projects are custom quotes since each customer and project is unique. **Custom quoting can be a valuable service to customers since it is done to meet their unique needs!** Make sure to include factors for Cost of Goods Sold (or COGS, which is all the direct costs of providing a service or product), overhead (many small businesses ignore this HUGE factor) and desired profit margin (you need to make money, not just break even!). Seek the help of a CPA or accounting professional to confirm how to calculate these factors.

Justifying what may seem as higher prices for services requires that you build a reputation that builds trust, loyalty and sales.

GOING FORWARD

Chapter 14:
Knowing When to Call in Help

Confession: I'm a horrible cook. Maybe I should rephrase that. My cooking is edible, but not incredible. So when a holiday or celebration rolls around, I let professional chefs handle this chore and I make reservations at some top notch restaurants in the area. That way I can enjoy the meal, the holiday and the company of those I care about. What's ironic is that it's cheaper for me to go this route, too, since my kitchen is not well equipped in utensils or supplies, necessitating purchases that I normally wouldn't make.

So what does this have to do with a small business? In my years of owning a business, I have learned that calling in professional small business help has enabled me to concentrate on the things I do best and grow my business. But, admittedly, in the early going I struggled by doing things the DIY (Do It Yourself) way. In some ways, I didn't realize there was a better way. At other times, I suffered from superhero syndrome, believing I could handle everything. Then there was always the matter of not having the money to outsource.

Knowing when to call in the professionals can be a difficult decision for many small business owners and entrepreneurs. Having a list of questions can help.

Questions To Help Make An Outsourcing Decision

Here are several questions to help make the decision of whether to enlist outside help:

1. *Do I have the necessary skills and/or experience?* Careful here! Solopreneurs and micro businesses can easily fall into the mistrusting *"I'd rather do it myself"* or superhero *"I can do it all"* traps, ignoring that they may not have the capability or capacity to do certain tasks for their businesses or clients.

2. *Do I have the time to continue doing this task?* How many hours per day/week/month/year do I spend on this task that I could be spending on sales or growing my business? Every hour that is spent on administrative, service or operational tasks is one that is not spent seeking or creating new sources of income. For example, I used to spend two to three days doing my monthly bookkeeping tasks. When I hired an excellent bookkeeping service, that was reduced to a couple hours per month, giving me more time to spend doing what I do best.

3. *Would an outside perspective be helpful?* Those who own their own businesses are sometimes too close to the operation to see the glaring problems. Because small business owners and entrepreneurs are often emotionally invested in their businesses too, this scenario can become even more problematic. While friends and family can be supportive, seeking an expert outsider's opinion can be more constructive.

4. *Is the task at hand outside my core area of expertise?* Many fields have subcategories that are almost separate fields within themselves. One example is

marketing consulting which could encompass ad design, distribution, email marketing, Internet advertising and so much more. If any subcategories are not areas of competence for the business, consider outsourcing the work to experts.

5. **How much would hiring outside help cost versus the cost to do it myself?** Especially when a business is new, funds can be tight. So new business owners are more inclined to "wear a lot of hats." One way to help avoid getting stuck in these non-revenue producing tasks is to build outside help costs into the budget right from the start. Owners also need to consider that their time has a dollar value attached to it. Every hour spent in non-growth or non-sales activities is spending money, not making money.

The Project From Hell

As I began to grow and expand my marketing business, one of the related areas that I considered adding was graphic design. I know my way around design programs such as Adobe Illustrator and my skills are okay. Yes, just okay. But with the market I served, I thought I'd be able to provide an acceptable level of service for the kinds of projects they would need.

Then came the project from hell.

One of my clients wanted to do a slick marketing package. I worked up a couple of designs which were, um, not exactly what they were looking for. So I kept pitching designs—about 10 in all and easily about 40+ hours of work. The client didn't go with any of them and put the project on the back burner. Translation: I didn't get paid. Actually, I was relieved. I was getting tired and frustrated and even hoped they'd decide to go with someone else.

Later on, the project was resurrected. But this time, it was different.

In the meantime, and as a result of the nightmare I had just experienced, I set out on a quest to find some graphic design partners. And I found a really good one... actually more than one! Not super expensive, but not bargain basement either.

So when the client resurrected this project from the back burner, I invited my graphic design friends into the meeting and informed the client that they will be handling all major design work for me going forward. In fact, I turned the whole project over to the design crew. The designers came back with three concepts and the client loved one of them.

Result? Happy client. Happy design firm who got a new, and continuing, client. And I look like an expert who has great connections, even if I didn't gain the sale.

Sometimes getting help means letting go. In this story, I got help for my business (and my client) and didn't have to pay a dime or time for it.

Going Forward

As we come to the end of our discussion on small business failures, I hope that you have discovered ways to rethink your situation and put yourself and your business on the road to success. Thank you for reading!

Add Heidi to Your Network!

Dr. Heidi Thorne, MBA/DBA, is an author and business speaker who focuses on small business and marketing topics. She has over 25 years of experience in sales, advertising, marketing and public relations, including a decade in the hospitality and trade show industries. As well, she was a trade newspaper editor for over 15 years, has blogged since 2010 and taught at the college level for five years.

Books. Heidi has written several books and eBooks on business and self publishing. For a current listing of all books, with links to purchase, visit the "Books" page at HeidiThorne.com.

Speaking. Need a speaker for your business event? Let Heidi engage and entertain your audience! For video previews and current topics, visit the "Speaking" page at HeidiThorne.com.

www.ingramcontent.com/pod-product-compliance
Lightning Source LLC
Chambersburg PA
CBHW060409190526
45169CB00002B/815